PERCEPTIONS AND REALITIES
FOR 21ST CENTURY LEADERS

IS IT WHAT YOU HOPED FOR?

JACK CORBIN GETZ

Charleston, SC
www.PalmettoPublishing.com

Is It What You Hoped For?
Copyright © 2022 by Jack Corbin Getz

All rights reserved
No portion of this book may be reproduced, stored in a retrieval system, or transmitted in any form by any means–electronic, mechanical, photocopy, recording, or other–except for brief quotations in printed reviews, without prior permission of the author.

First Edition

Paperback: 979-8-88590-110-9
eBook: 979-8-88590-111-6

What some say about the book.

"Excellent work. A really good and easy to absorb look at the roles and cost of leadership. Congratulations!"

"This book would be a great addition/resource to an intro to business class. It identifies all the necessary qualities needed to be an effective leader and clearly illustrates the give and take of the freedom, autonomy, increased compensation, and responsibility that come with upward movement in a corporation."

"It would be a valuable read to those who wish to climb the corporate ladder if one, as you say, desires to do so."

Dedication:

To Those Who Lead

TABLE OF CONTENTS

Foreword i
Introduction. v

Chapter One - Perilous Times 1
Chapter Two - Historical Perspectives of
Leadership 7
Chapter Three - Leadership Minimums 15
Chapter Four - Building A Leadership Legacy. . . . 45
Chapter Five - Motivations 51
Chapter Six - The Pyramid: Why Organizations
Attract Leaders Pyramid - Part One 65
Chapter Seven - Leadership Perceptions and
Realities: Why Organizations Attract Leaders
Pyramid - Part Two 75

Summary and Conclusion 87
Acknowledgements 95

FOREWORD

"*Business Insider* published a poll in October 2020 saying a majority of Americans believed the U.S. was *already* in the midst of a "cold" civil war. Then last fall, the University of Virginia Center for Politics released a poll finding that a majority of people who had voted to reelect former President Donald Trump in 2020 now wanted their state to secede from the Union.

"The UVA data also showed a stunning 41% of those who voted for Joe Biden in 2020 also said it might now be "time to split the country."[1]"

It does not take much to accept the dire conclusions reached by these studies. I open with them not to comment on the political divide in America today, but to springboard from it into the theme of this book. WHY

---
1   https://www.npr.org/2022/01/11/1071082955/imagine-another-american-civil-war-but-this-time-in-every-state?utm_source=facebook&utm_medium=news_tab

do people want to become leaders in today's turbulent political and social climate, routinely walking a razor thin line between great success and complete personal ruin? Leaders today appear in the crosshairs of a fickle, unseen enemy who enjoys nothing more than the routine destruction of society.

Like the historical statues that are disappearing from our cultural heritage, important leaders are being cancelled regularly for things they may have done or said in their youth. Accusations are often as good as a trial and leaders are permanently disgraced for relatively minor mistakes or slip ups they made along the way. "America is stuck in this crazy cycle because it has a public square in which basic truths everyone knew until yesterday are being made unsayable."[2]

Those who lead today are targeted more viciously than ever, and truthfully, I find myself grateful that my days of leadership have ended. Now, if still in the game, I would not want to lead. I would want to run for cover.

Certainly I am not suggesting this is the first society to face such deep divisions. People seeking advantage over others is part of the human psyche. In the book

---

2   NyPost.com. Douglas Murray. March 26, 2022.

of Genesis, Cain and Abel were virtually alone in the world yet they found a way to create an animus that led to the first recorded murder.

The most difficult times in history, however, seem to produce some of the most powerful and effective leaders. Simply listing the names of both legendary and infamous individuals reminds us that no era is without its challenges at least as perilous as ours.

It is important to understand that legendary leadership is not reserved for political or business leaders alone but for everyone who finds themself *called* or *conscripted* to lead. Football coaches are leaders, as are pastors, teachers, parents, business owners, generals, sergeants and corporals. It may sound overly obvious, but virtually everyone is a leader in some way, if only of themself.

Ultimately, *Perceptions and Realities* about the allure of leadership in this unique period of time is what this abbreviated book is about.

Finally, this book focuses on the general maxims of leadership that apply to institutions, both big and small business, not-for-profits, government, schools, community organizations, churches and the military. That said, the challenge of finding words describing such a diverse grouping led me to use labels not intended as specific, but universal. Words like "business", "organization", "group" etc. are not intended for any single sector of the wide world of leadership, but to include all who lead in any capacity or setting.

INTRODUCTION

NOVICE JOURNALISTS ARE taught to answer six rudimentary questions about any story: Who? What? When? Where? Why? and How? In this newest addition to the universal leadership library I will purposefully sidestep five of those questions, particularly HOW, and focus on WHY people want to be leaders. Discovering motivations behind why so many desire to lead may be more helpful than producing yet another book on HOW to lead.

The birth of this book took place a few months back while my wife and I were on a long road trip. As we chatted, a familiar subject came up: our extreme discomfort about the way the world is now. I innocently asked her, "Who in their right mind would want to be a leader today?" With that, my mind eventually led me to the idea that despite the times, leadership is still desired by many, as if drawn by a magnet toward the top.

I was a leader during much less stressful times. My climb to the top was motivated by the notion that gaining some degree of autonomy and authority brought reduced stress and more perks. I worked long hours, every day, including weekends. I carried the responsibility of dealing with unending personnel issues, budget shortfalls, frustrating expectations while trying to maintain my equilibrium surrounded by sycophants.

That said, we watch friends now facing the challenges of 21st century leadership and wonder how they can survive. The popular gamesmanship of saying that kids today have it so much better than we did is simply not true. I do not covet the unique challenges facing today's leaders for one minute.

We have watched blow after blow hailed on them from both inside and outside their organizations, and while good and capable leaders, I wonder if they still believe the various compensations for being the top dog are as good as they thought they would be.

"In the last year, job openings soared and record levels of worker turnover shifted the balance of power to the worker."[3] Leadership today may be likened to when the Hebrew slaves were expected to produce the same

---

3   marketwatch.com Quentin Fottrell. The Best Job in America.

amount of bricks with a reduced supply of straw. The things leaders once depended on - public goodwill, eager talent arriving, organizational/professional respect, and predictable funding practices - are suddenly up for grabs. Management assumptions from only a few years ago are gone and new paradigms must be created to survive.

One-time pillars of the community like the Catholic Church, the Boy Scouts of America and The Salvation Army have all been targeted, sometimes justly, by a secular society that no longer considers their values relevant. Their flaws are all that surface and their innate goodness is ignored by the crazed mob who wants to tear down more anachronistic statues and replace them with chaos.

The pyramid graphic you will see later is a visual description of why people in any business, charity, church, school or government agency still think they want to ascend the leadership pyramid. Some will always believe the top is a better place to be, and many find that it is, but can they honestly say *it is what they hoped for?*

Chapter One

PERILOUS TIMES

WATCHING THE NEWS on television was something I used to do…incessantly, bordering on fanaticism. When things were going my way, or my side was doing well at villainizing the bad guys, I was happy. Then the tables turned about a year ago and the media people I trusted proved unworthy of my trust, and those I continued to follow were delivering such bad news that I chose to crawl into my media hole trying to de-stress and regain a sense of mental equilibrium. My values, my country and my emotional well-being were shifting seismically under my feet and pulling the media plug was the only way to ensure that I could begin my internal, emotional and spiritual healing. I was once sure that, like Superman, America would always pursue "truth, justice and the American way". I am doubting that is still true.

Yet any competent historian will easily recognize that truth has always been elusive, and every historical era faced the same basic question with which we wrestle today: Who can we trust?

Today, instead of blindly obeying the church, the king or the even latest strong man, we are in the grip of Post Modern political realities which challenge old comfortable values with new unsettling ideas and realities. No police? No gender? No faith? Really?

Our current crisis is the Covid pandemic which broadsided the world like a large truck running a red light. It arrived just before another highly divisive presidential election. The stakes for both sides seemed unusually high, but again, a good historical search will reveal that divisive elections are often the norm, not the exception. Emotions were high and accusations of corruption from each side created unsettling protests; in some cases unfortunate violence erupted across the nation. Added to this, racial tensions resurfaced creating the notion that another civil war is indeed a possibility.

There is little middle ground for debate or disagreement. Distrust, false information, and a pervasive mistrust of authority - and media - led to a palpable crisis of truth, and a vacuum of public trust. "Government leaders and journalists are considered the least trustworthy societal leaders, according to Edelman's new 2022 global "Trust Barometer," a survey of 35,000 respondents across 28 countries.

- A majority of people globally believe journalists (67%), government leaders (66%) and business executives (63%) are "purposely trying to mislead people by saying things they know are false or gross exaggerations."
- Around the world, people fear the media is becoming more sensational for commercial gain and that government leaders continue to exploit divisions for political gain."[4]

Countless millions internalized the strife as forms of anarchy were seen on the news. Then the second unnoticed pandemic of this era blossomed in the form of mass depression and anxiety. Americans internalized the stress; many, like me, dropped out, lost confidence in authority, entered camps of similar individuals who all fruitlessly longed for a reset button just to discover who we were again, what we had become, and what bombshell was coming next.

---

[4] AXIOS.com Sara Fischer. "Distrust in political, media and business leaders sweeps the globe." 2022

There may be no greater paradigm shift - and subsequent challenge - to any society than when the public loses faith in leaders, media sources of information, or major institutions to present the truth. We used to believe we knew where to go to get truth. But in today's age of social media, blogs, and search websites with instant information, true or not, we simply find a media champion who represents our values, and we side with them. Today the two camps of public discourse agree that the news media has lost its way and turned from truth reporting to political activism.

We older folks used to trust the news reported by Huntley-Brinkley, John Chancellor and the man voted most credible in America at the time, Walter Cronkite. Today, the voices of news have become shrill, angry and fearfully biased toward their political leanings.

This distrust of authority seeps into every part of society and the crisis of truth could be the thing that destroys or changes America the most. Or so it seems. Truthfully, as unraveled as our social order is today, there have been other eras of unrest and anarchy that seemed every bit as terminal to our national values and security as those we witness today.

As a nation, America survived a Civil War, two World Wars, the Cold War, the Cuban Missile Crisis, assassinations, bombings, 911, rioting and tragic mass shootings. As a people we have developed some thick skin. Yet despite the deep fault lines we see today, we remain one nation, not likely under God, or indivisible, but we are still viable and capable of being productive and beneficent toward each other. To do that, we would be wise to embrace an elongated *Selah* - a thoughtful break - to regain our focus and hope.

I find myself pitying those individuals who either want to, or find themselves placed in positions of leadership today. It is a world characterized by the image of quicksand. Every comment, action, or opinion is scrutinized so that even small stumbles or long past indiscretions can lead to public humiliation, and in some cases, to organizational demise.

Leadership today is uniquely fraught with disaster, fueled as never before by the ubiquitous presence of cameras, cell phones, quick-hit public media forums and false information, all of which can be deadly for both the guilty and the innocent. Incendiary words are banned and merely saying them can destroy lives. Even saying something that is true but unpopular can lead to being "cancelled" by faceless and unaccountable social inquisitors. Grace and flexibility are not overused commodities in the world today.

Has leadership always been so dangerous and consequential or am I overreacting to our current situation? One way to know is to look back to other perilous times and see what we can learn from several notable leaders.

Chapter Two

HISTORICAL PERSPECTIVES OF LEADERSHIP

I MANAGED RECENTLY to listen to well over 50 hours of Winston Churchill's epic *History of the English Speaking Peoples.* It is a comprehensive historical work presented in his unparalleled writing skill. The work details a millennium of Britain's national development. In it, the underlying stories of leadership sublimate all other topics. Sometimes it is directly mentioned and other times it is silently present, but it is never far from the mind of the writer.

In the 16th century Henry VIII's frustration with his inability to produce a suitable male heir (a leadership issue) led him to take matters into his own hands, leading to his excommunication by the pope. Remember, only a few years prior to this crisis, the pope bestowed the title Defender of the Faith to a devout and devoted Henry. But as circumstances conspired against him, Henry ignored the unthinkable punishment, brushing it aside as a mere impediment to his need to produce a son. "Henry had exhausted his options for remarrying within the church and decided excommunication was a fair price to pay for independence from the pope and the potential of fathering an heir."[5]

By these, and other drastic actions, Henry allowed the previously unthinkable English reformation to take root, producing the birth of the Anglican Church. If one did not know the history, one might assume the creation of a new English national church was the result of something more noble than producing a male heir. But all of history at this time ultimately boiled down to leadership.

I am distressed thinking about the number of conscripted citizen soldiers who died horrible deaths over the issues of future leadership. Both the War of the Roses and the 100 Years' War were sparked by the question of who had the right to lead England.

---

5   history.com Pope Clement VII forbids King Henry VIII from remarrying. 1/05/2022.

Leadership in this period was never an historical footnote but the primary shaper of Western Civilization. The prime mover, Henry VIII, was an incredibly expedient and pragmatic leader, to a fault. He responded to the perils of his time without fear of temporal or eternal consequences, which was the only way he knew how to lead. His forceful ways led to great tragedy for his friends, his family, his followers and his piece of the world, and in the end his willfulness and failure inadvertently produced one of the great monarchs of history, Queen Elizabeth I.

Henry is one example of a leader operating in evolutionary times. His checkered legacy suggests that some leaders want to lead primarily so they can control circumstances to suit their needs. Absolute monarchs have an advantage over those who must lead by consensus, not coercion.

Later when political power shifted away from monarchs to parliaments and other citizen-driven bodies, ministers were chosen by the majority party to lead with the consent of the common man. Rarely did a new leader inherit a peaceful and prosperous nation, and change was always the result of dissatisfaction or trouble.

The newly chosen leaders were often greeted by financial shortfalls, unfriendly neighbors, belligerent rivals and unsettled constituents. In truth, leadership was never a gift to cherish, but a burden to be borne, yet men, and a few remarkable women, continued to fight for the right to lead.

Winston Churchill's climb to prominence took place during the ominous days preceding WW II. Who in their right mind would want to assume the leadership for a nation about to be attacked by the unstoppable Nazi Blitzkrieg? Hitler's troops, tanks, planes and panzers were rampaging across Europe and Africa with impudence, and Britain was on his hit list. To make things worse, their allies were already subsumed, critical supplies and equipment were unavailable, the United States was uncommitted leaving England ill-prepared to fight a war for its survival. Now those were tough times.

The prime minister, Neville Chamberlain, was dedicated to keeping peace through appeasement, and Hitler was happy to play along, growing his war machine unopposed. It was quickly evident that appeasement was a fatal policy to pursue with Germany, so Winston Churchill, feeling he had the right stuff, persistently maneuvered himself into position to undertake the colossal challenge of saving the free world from the schemes of the Third Reich. WHY?

Against all odds, Churchill eagerly longed to lead Britain away from Chamberlain's appeasement strategy toward the defense of not only his homeland, but also against the assault of freedom and democracy in the world. His toolbox included a family heritage of leadership, a bulldog tenacity and temperament, a history of governmental involvement and a rock-solid conviction that he was the man of the hour. He understood the cost of victory, and oddly, he was able to sell the idea that sacrifice, courage and optimism in this dark hour seemed reasonable to a frightened nation. Fortunately, Churchill wanted to be a leader, and thankfully he was the perfect fit for that time in history.

I surmise that both he and Henry VIII were men of destiny who decided the enemy of their values was not invincible, but subject to their abilities to lead despite overwhelming circumstances. We remember them, and others, as overcomers who would never yield to any enemy. We do not remember or honor the names of those who faced tough times and gave up. They serve instead as examples of how not to lead.

Several useful leadership principles emerge from studying history. Great leaders never give up. They find the silver lining in the clouds. They articulate their values, motivate their constituents and share the secrets of their vision. Listen to how Churchill galvanized a nation and overcame his political enemies with this short but dynamic commitment: "We shall defend our island, whatever the cost may be, we shall fight on the beaches, we shall fight on the landing grounds, we shall fight in the fields and in the streets, we shall fight in the hills; we shall never surrender."

Churchill's only true peer in the world at that time was American president Franklin Roosevelt. Both men led their countries during the most perilous of times, Churchill primarily as a stubborn, hope-generating war leader and Roosevelt as an optimistic social reformer. Upon his death "Millions of Americans mourned the death of the man who led the United States through two of the greatest crises of the 20th century: the Great Depression and World War II."[6] "When Roosevelt took office on March 4, 1933, most banks were closed, farms were suffering, 13 million workers were unemployed, and industrial production stood at just over half its 1929 level."[7] Both men's monumental challenges boggle the modern mind. Yet for some reason, each was determined to carry the leadership torch during the world's darkest hours.

We will see other historical examples of leadership in the following pages, mostly as they relate to the skills required to navigate through tough waters. But now let

---

6   history.com. March 4, 2022
7   Ibid

us consider how someone who wants to lead, despite the challenges, can prepare themselves to overcome the obstacles to their success. The legendary Indiana basketball coach, Bobby Knight, knew how to win, and his words set us up perfectly for the next chapter: "The will to succeed is important, but what's more important is the will to prepare."

Chapter Three

LEADERSHIP MINIMUMS

WITHOUT ENTERING THE complicated and vastly oversubscribed topic of HOW to lead, I have selected ten attributes that focus on the nature and character of leaders who *want* to lead effectively tomorrow. The list is not about the science of leadership, but the art.

These demanding qualities may, for the unprepared, serve as warning signs that leadership never comes cheap. As the venerable coach Lou Holtz says, "Winners embrace hard work. They love the discipline of it, the trade-off they're making to win. Losers, on the other hand, see it as punishment. And that's the difference." Adding further to this foundational leadership principle are the sagely words of the late Secretary of State, General Colin Powell, "There are no secrets to success.

It is the result of preparation, hard work, and learning from failure."[8]

I recently heard someone say the ability to learn is the most important quality a leader can have. The importance of honing these skills cannot be overstated, but the ability to communicate them through credible and consistent action is better. Many credit St. Francis of Assisi with the valuable axiom: "Preach the gospel at all times. Use words when necessary." That mantra worked well for him, and I believe it will for those who routinely demonstrate their key values, leading from their strengths. "A leader is one who knows the way, goes the way, and shows the way."[9]

"So how do we encourage the next generation toward greatness rather than simply promoting compromise, concession, and conformity…? The answer is to train them in a solid set of convictions, strong enough to be worth dying for and poignant enough to be worth defending when no one else will."[10]

Called and Qualified

To be effective, a leader must possess an innate urge/need to be one. Some believe the appropriate word for

---

[8] 1440 Daily Digest, April, 5, 2022.
[9] John C. Maxwell
[10] Annie Holmquist https://www.intellectualtakeout.org/where-have-all-the-great-men-gone---not-to-harvard-/

that urge is calling. Callings have a mysterious side to them because they imply a superior someone or something is issuing the invitation. The notion of divine calling is a popular feature throughout the Bible. One might mention a familiar name in either Testament and assume there is a calling story associated with it. Other world religions also feature persons who responded to mysterious urgings to lead and new world faiths were born.

That said, there are also non-spiritual leadership urges that are a compelling response to an important need or cause. I felt a sense of calling to be a teacher. My sister felt a sense of calling to be a nurse. My wife sensed a calling to be a counselor. My first daughter can comfortably speak about her calling to be a speech therapist.

The stories relating to people seeing a need and meeting it, and pursuing the means to address it, are as plentiful and diverse as there are people. It would take a separate book to tell even a small percentage of the stories associated with need-driven, not self-motivated, callings.

The truth is that any calling must be balanced by competence. A calling to be a lifeguard is not enough. One must be certified before they can be trusted with a whistle. Clearly, calling without competence is merely an emotion, or dream, not a credential. Sometimes an exaggerated perception of one's capacity to lead seeps into the minds of some individuals. They claim to be chosen or called to lead because they view leadership as a desirable package of power, privilege and perks. So why not claim it?

Truthfully, leadership is far less about an esoteric calling than a pragmatic response to achieve the goal. As we go along in this book, we will see that leadership uses a multitude of qualities in addition to desire. Leadership is a place of trust granted to those who demonstrate a consistent record of desired achievements. Calling is a noble sense of destiny but it's merely fool's gold without a body of good and consistent results to make it relevant.

Napoleon Bonaparte was a young ambitious lieutenant in the French army when he came upon a line of canons directed at the enemy. Stepping out from his role as an observer, he suggested that the commander's guns were aligned incorrectly if he hoped to disable the enemy. At first the commander was indignant toward the brash, slight young officer but he soon saw the reason behind the suggestion and wisely realigned his canons. Then the commander watched with amazement as the new trajectory was perfect, and the foe was routed.

Because of his audacious behavior and subsequent success, this unknown upstart, Napoleon Bonaparte, was soon called upon to lead a much more crucial assault, again with great success. Before long he was commissioned as commander of the French army. With his phenomenal success - and capacity backing up his words with actions - the Pope crowned him as emperor of Europe, a role he fulfilled for almost twenty years. He enjoyed leadership and once said: "I can no longer obey; I have tasted command, and I cannot give it up." Napoleon's sense of calling to lead worked for him because he coupled it with successful leadership skills.

> **Lesson:** *Calling means very little without the capacity to fulfill it.*

Creative and Resourceful

When I met someone through my work, I was always friendly, but I was also quietly opportunistic. I knew that being on the lookout for those lucky individuals who might one day help me do my job better was part of my mission.

When resources are difficult to obtain, a good leader must always be a good recruiter and talent scout. While that might sound mercenary, every effective leader understands my meaning. Analyzing resources is a creative means to an end. I once met a retired man who loved driving so I let him pursue his passion, asking him to drive for our community organization, and his help was invaluable. Another time I met someone in a coffee shop and after a few minutes of conversation I discovered he was a painter. Before long he volunteered to paint our community service building if I provided the paint. But please remember that this strategy must always be a win/win to ensure that it's resourcefulness not manipulation.

A resourceful leader knows they can not do everything themself so to excel they surround themself with people better than themselves. The great basketball coach John Wooden understood the value of iron sharpening iron when he said, "Whatever you do in life, surround yourself with smart people who'll argue with you."

Abraham Lincoln famously chose his cabinet by inviting several of his biggest critics to play key roles in his government. He knew they were jealous of his success and it is reported each believed themselves superior leaders to him. Despite that, he said, "We needed the strongest men of the party in the cabinet...I had looked the party over and concluded that these were the very strongest men....I had no right to deprive the country of their services."[11] The effective leader under-

---

11   https://presidentlincoln.illinois.gov/Resources/699d8db2-7d4d-4abc-928e-fcdcfd01500f/lincolns-cabinet-rivalry-respect.pdf

stands how to identify talent, how to motivate different personalities and skill types, how to communicate the mission and how to skillfully use accountability to lead efficiently.

A friend who was a highly effective leader once told me they did not hire solely by qualifications, or even by character, but by versatility. "I want athletes more than specialists," he once told me. I immediately understood his point. We both believed that the versatile person can quickly learn specific skills and practices, but they can also contribute to the larger good because of their ability to understand their best contribution to the organization was their capacity to adapt and fill multiple needs. Their strength is their willingness to respond to any circumstance with excellence and play the hand they are given.

Certainly credentials and experience are important and often required, but leaders with creativity and resourcefulness who incorporate both traditional and non-traditional approaches to management usually win the day.

> **Lesson:** *If you never ask, you will never know.*

Committed and Credible

I believe the level of a leader's commitment is one of the first things followers recognize. Most people will determine their own level of involvement in the mission through the parameters and example set by the leader. We have all seen movies where the king sits on top a distant ridge surrounded by his personal guards and billowing banners while he motions his army to attack on his behalf.

I recently read a story about Queen Elizabeth I's heroic leadership in facing overwhelming odds in the battle against the Spanish Armada. Similar to the scene in the film *Braveheart* where William Wallace inspired his troops to give all for Scotland, young Elizabeth donned her armor and rode to her vastly outnumbered troops, urging them to fight to the death for England. What made her charge effective was her promise that she would be there with them in battle and die, if necessary.

The stakes were that high. Their queen was ready to die with them, and unlike less heroic leaders, she was good to her word. She stayed with them, and thanks to some helpful shifts in the weather, her army and navy responded by overcoming immense odds and saving England from defeat. From that point on, her leadership was irrevocably established and none ever questioned either her commitment or her credibility again.

It is one thing to give orders, but it is only the great leader who engenders commitment in others because their words and actions align perfectly. That's the meaning of credibility. Bosses do not always have to get their hands dirty, but they do need to demonstrate they are in the game, playing their part and inspiring commitment in those they hope to lead.

Lesson: *Involved leading always trumps distant commanding.*

Commanding and Decisive

The ability to command is critical to effective and inspiring leadership. Imagine that king on the hill or a queen with the troops finishing a pep talk with, "I sure hope I'm right about this."

To command effectively, one needs to be able to discern the circumstances and adapt methods to match the need. The ability to read the moment is not something every leader can do. Decisions may sometimes be mulled over but often they cannot. In stressful or chaotic moments the best leaders bring stability and calm, even though they may be saying to themselves, "I sure hope I'm right about this."

There are times when a commanding presence is required, but that weapon is one best sheathed until necessary. Perhaps the key to command is selling the notion that what you say is credible and worthy of trust. "Your position never gives you the right to command. It only imposes on you the duty of so living your life that others can receive your orders without being humiliated."[12]

Great leaders do their homework and seek good counsel every day so they do not have to wing it very often. They also understand that their inability to make consistently good choices based in sound reasoning will create damaging consequences for themselves and those they lead.

Lesson: *If you shoot at nothing you will surely hit it, but hitting the target takes practice and so does command.*

---

12 Dag Hammarskjold

Capable and Productive

Walt Disney knew something about turning capacity into production. He also appears on the Mount Rushmore of people who turned dreams into realities. He said, "A person should set goals as early as they can and devote all their energy to getting there."[13]

The two qualities of capacity and productivity go hand in hand. They play off each other producing a result that is indispensable to great leaders. Why? Because without one, you will not get the other.

If you have a child's plastic beach shovel you will not be able to move mountains. If you have limited capacity, you will have limited productivity. If that is true, the leader's priorities must always include increasing capacity. Reading, schooling, asking questions, listening more than talking, experimenting, and watching everything that happens in the workplace builds capacity and only capacity leads to productivity.

Remember, we learn more by doing, not just hearing. The greater the involvement in the learning process, the greater the retention. Effective educators tell us that we remember only five percent of what we hear, ten

---

13   Walt Disney.

percent of what we read, seventy five percent of what we do, and ninety percent of what we teach to others. [14]

One final life lesson is that often failure is the best instructor. Every great inventor has a mountain of failures before they find success. Both Albert Einstein, the physicist, and Sir Francis Bacon, the father of modern science, were mediocre students as children. They endured their failures, learned from their mistakes, persevered and carved out places as the two of the greatest scientists who over lived.

Steve Jobs suggests the importance of both capability and productivity saying: "Be a yardstick of quality. Some people aren't used to an environment where excellence is expected."

Lesson: *If you want a bigger shovel, prove you know how to handle a smaller one first.*

Responsible and Resilient

The connection between responsibility and resilience may elude some at first, but they both tap the root of

---

14 Thepeakperformancecenter.com. The Learning Pyramid.

maturity as their source of power. If one leads, they will either learn to be resilient or will take a Humpty Dumpty fall. The ability to take a hit, learn from it, grow and go on is possibly the best definition of maturity I know of. I often say that maturity is doing what needs to be done, even when it isn't fun.

Because the leader is the face of the company or organization, when things go wrong, the arrows point at them. Coach Nick Saban clearly understands the value of resilience: "One thing about championship teams is that they're resilient. No matter what is thrown at them, no matter how deep the hole, they find a way to bounce back and overcome adversity."

Responsibility is a word loaded with meaning. When bisected the two words that appear are response and ability. Response is sometimes confused with another word, react, but they are more opposites than synonyms. Responding is a function of the mind while reacting is a product of emotion. *Responses* are grounded in logic, information and judgement. *Reactions* are usually emotionally driven by circumstance so they are not always appropriate in serious settings.

The key lesson here is that leaders must learn to respond, not react, and great leaders develop the ability to respond responsibly. We teach children, pets, employees and husbands to be responsible as part of their maturation process. Responsibility is not a gift; it is an acquired skill. It takes time to learn the value of being responsible. It is a key that unlocks the next door in life.

One good reason children aren't allowed to get a driver's license or drink beer is they have yet to develop their sense of judgement. They aren't responsible enough to make good choices about things that are potentially dangerous. They need to learn that there are consequences for being irresponsible.

Responsible people learn how to be resilient. Like responsibility, resilience is not a gift but a practiced skill and eventually a good habit. Not everyone is mature enough to be a leader, possibly because they never learned to adjust to setbacks by responding, not reacting. Resisting a police officer over a speeding ticket could quickly reveal the biggest difference between a *response* and a *reaction*.

Resilient leaders understand that criticism is part of their unwritten job description. W.C. Fields captured the essence of this truth comedically quipping: "I would not have had anything to eat if it wasn't for the stuff the audience threw at me." Vincent Van Gogh once said about the value of resilience, "Success is sometimes the outcome of a whole string of failures." And Dr. Robert Schuller's optimistic outlook on life reveals another important aspect of resilient people: "Tough times never last. Tough people do." And finally, Coach John Wooden supports this principle: "You can't let praise or criticism get to you. It's a weakness to get caught up in either one."

Some learn too late that a responsible leader must expect criticism - even for doing the right thing. And those who emotionally *react to others,* instead of maturely *responding* - spend too much of their leadership capital repairing damaged relationships. Resilient leaders understand the adage: "I never lose. I either win or learn."

Early in life I learned the importance of resilience from my favorite singer, Nat King Cole. The truth found in the Dorothy Fields' lyrics, written in 1936 during the Great Depression, a time when almost everyone was trying to get back on their feet, still resonates today:

> Nothing's impossible I have found,
> For when my chin is on the ground,
> I pick myself up,
> Dust myself off,
> Start All over again.
> Don't lose your confidence if you slip,
> Be grateful for a pleasant trip,

And pick yourself up,
Dust yourself off,
Start all over again.
Work like a soul inspired,
Till the battle of the day is won.
You may be sick and tired,
But you'll be a man, my son!
Will you remember the famous men,
Who had to fall to rise again?
So take a deep breath,
Pick yourself up,
Dust yourself off,
Start all over again.[15]

Lesson: *Pick yourself up, dust yourself off, start all over again.*

Reasonable and Open

I once had a coworker who was management level in a large not-for-profit organization. He was famous for saying no to anything brought to him for approval. He did not directly affect much of my work, so I asked him

---

15 PICK YOURSELF UP
    From the Film: Swing Time 1936
    (Lyrics by: Dorothy Fields / Music by: Jerome Kern)
    Fred Astaire & Ginger Rogers

about his rationale. He bristled, as he often did, and literally said, "I always say no to any request the first time because it weeds out the weak from the strong. If they really want it, they will come back." It should go without saying that a leader who desires to motivate and lead effectively must be reasonable and open to others not a tyrant who enjoys watching people deflate before their eyes.

Recently, I had lunch with the regional director for Goodwill Industries and during our conversation I asked if he wanted to meet someone I thought might be useful to his mission. With a big smile and widening eyes he immediately answered "Yes! I want to meet everyone!" He was open to receiving input from others and his remarkable leadership was largely driven by a desire to expand his circle of influence as wide as possible.

Another time I had a similar conversation with a man who was a home remodeler. I asked if he wanted to meet the affable guy who was building our new house. I assumed they might have something in common, but his answer, possibly in jest, surprised me: "No. Why would I want to meet a competitor?" John Cook, Nebraska's iconic five-time national champion women's volleyball coach "…has learned to lessen his own load by trusting and delegating more, rather than trying to control everything. Bottomline, he thinks, coaches [leaders] today must be masters of adaptation."[16]

Good leaders are open to new ideas, new voices, new partnerships and new ways to grow. They are rarely unreasonably guarded, unavailable, negative or isolated. Instead they are willing to listen, adjust to circumstances, examine the rules and develop a sense of approachability. It takes time to create a climate of confidence and comfort in any organization, but there is a huge return on any investment to those who are open and accessible to their charges.

Lesson: *It's better to know some of the questions than all the answers.*[17]

Pragmatic and Accomplished

I believe pragmatism is the most direct road to accomplishment. Pragmatic leaders are those who believe there is always another way to achieve the desired end, and while the cost at times may be high, pragmatism is the means to productivity and desired change. Pragmatism is the antidote to routine, cliche and dogma. It is all too

---

16 https://klin.com/2022/04/22/john-cook-knows-darkness-hes-located-the-light/

17 James Thurber

easy to follow "the way we have always done it" or to be mired in methods proven inefficient and ineffective.

Pragmatists produce, but often they are not popular with those who are frozen in process. It is quite simple. If that mountain is in the way, we will go around it, or through it if necessary, but we will not settle here and do nothing. Pragmatism sees a need and fills it; senses an opportunity and pursues it; understands reality and embraces it.

An optimist sees a glass of water as half full. A pessimist sees the glass as half empty. A pragmatist drinks the water.

Possibly the greatest (and worst?) example of a leader being pragmatic is President Harry Truman dropping nuclear bombs on Hiroshima and Nagasaki. He based his decision that bombing those cities was the best way to end the ongoing suffering caused by the seemingly endless war.

Has there ever been a more difficult decision made in history? It is certainly easy in hindsight to say it was the wrong decision, but at the time the pragmatic choice was to sacrifice some to save many. President Truman's pragmatism is clearly seen in his comment, "The atom bomb was no 'great decision.' It was merely another powerful weapon in the arsenal of righteousness."

Obviously, there are rules that cannot be broken without severe consequences, but the pragmatist weighs the value of the rule versus the accomplishment and finds a way forward, or dies trying. Not every decision requires pragmatic leadership, but when those tough nuts pop up, the pragmatist will find a way to crack them and get to the good stuff. Even Larry the Cable Guy's "Git 'er done" mantra speaks to the methodology of the pragmatic leader.

Pragmatists are driven by logic and strategy not emotion or tradition.

> **Lesson:** *"I will either find a way, or make one."* Hannibal

Teachable and Humble

Teachability and humility are two words that on the surface feel like passive traits, not strong leadership qualities. Good leaders cannot portray weakness or passivity, right? I say no, that is not right. Some things are not what they appear, and humility may be the best example of that truth.

My immediate image of humility is Mother Teresa. The slight founder of the Sisters of the Poor in Calcutta (Kolkata), India was a world celebrity, known by most, great and small. I have two favorite photos of her bowing with hands in a supplicant's prayer posture while in the presence of high profile people like the Pope or Princess Diana. But, true to character, she gave the same deference to the lowest in the caste system who she saw as representatives of her Lord Jesus.

When thinking of humble leaders, St. Paul may not be the first who comes to mind. Before his conversion he was a hard core zealot, a highly educated Pharisee, and an early leader of the Christian opposition movement in Israel. Divisiveness and arrogance characterized his life more than humility and teachability.

Even after Paul's spiritual awakening, he was as opinionated as a man could be. Today some misuse his words to decry Christianity as a bigoted and intolerant cult, not the source of love and compassion. But reading his letters reveals a man of strong conviction with clear and authoritative teachings. Yet despite his remarkable accomplishments, the seed of humility was growing inside him.

Paul once said, "Though I am the least deserving of all God's people, he graciously gave me the privilege of telling the Gentiles about the endless treasures available to them in Christ."[18] Paul was not blowing smoke

---

18 Ephesians 3:9. New Living Translation

when he said that. He was simply gauging himself at that stage in his new faith against those he considered more worthy of praise than he.

He was certainly not the least educated, nor the least articulate and certainly not the least intelligent but excelled in all these areas above everyone. He worked among the simple, mostly illiterate Christian converts, and was quite literally the *most* by comparison to normal standards of that day.

So what was Paul saying about himself? To understand him, listen to his words regarding the nature of humility: "Do not think of yourself more highly than you ought, but rather think of yourself with sober judgment, in accordance with the faith God has distributed to each of you."[19] His humility was real because he was judging himself on the scale of faith, not personal accomplishments. As a new Christian, he was now living by different standards than before. He was not the least of men, but he might have been the least among many other people of faith.

Paul knew who he was and was not bashful about sharing his pedigree, but here he was simply saying that we ought to be sober in our self appraisal, not

---

19 Romans 12:3 New International Version

self-deprecating when it is not warranted, but aware of both strengths and weaknesses. We may be superior to colleagues in some areas but clearly inferior in others. Arrogance suggests we are superior in all things. Humility is honestly understanding who we are and who we are not.

Humility is not thinking of yourself as less than others, but accurately discerning who you are, why you are here and how you can create a space where you empower others around you to thrive and grow. Humility is an accurate appraisal of who you are at this moment and responding in strength. It is not arrogant to say you are the best if you are and you can back it up. Both Mother Teresa and Paul were outliers, yet they considered themselves unworthy to be called great.

I happen to be a fairly good watercolor painter. After a lifetime of trying - and failing - I paint well enough to sell some of my work. At times I receive generous compliments from individuals saying I am gifted, a word I actively shun because once I had no talent at all. My "gift" had nothing to do with my art, but was a continuing desire to get better, something that motives me to this day.

I may bask in the glow of occasional adulation until I think about my teacher who is a world class artist. Yes,

I am good. I admit it. That is not arrogance but a illustration of how humility measures itself against higher standards. Comparing my best work to his worst is like a child with crayons competing with Michelangelo's Sistine Chapel.

Leaders who understand who they are will command the respect they require to lead others. "Every man I meet is in some way my superior; and in that I can learn of him.[20]" This quote from Emerson, among America's most renowned thought leaders, is both humbling and inspiring. Notice he did not say everyone was superior to him in "all" ways, just some. His words remind us that "…every human being has something to teach, and something to learn — and everyone can grow and evolve if they set aside ego, and, like Emerson, uncover new truths."[21]

My friend, a recently retired and successful international business leader, routinely met with heads of state and American government leaders in the course of selling his product. He made a lot of money, served on multiple boards, often as chair, and never let a good opportunity get past him. He had every reason to be content with his abilities and achievements. He was

---

20 "Think," Ralph Waldo Emerson
21 https://www.inspiringquotes.com/9-quotes-that-get-to-the-heart-of-transcendentalism

the recognized expert in his field, and his field was the whole world. Got it? Big dog.

One of the things he likes to do in retirement is call old friends and colleagues, reminiscing and sharing laughs and concerns. His son once asked him why he called so many people. His answer is obvious, if you know him, but a man of his stature does not often say things like "I call people I respect so I can learn from them". A humble person knows they can learn something from everyone. "If you're done learning, you're done growing."[22] I think that illustrates the principles of teachability and humility quite well.

Humility is simply knowing who you really are and understanding your rightful place. It is also being gracious toward others who may not share your expertise or level on the leadership ladder. Actively seeking to learn more every day, whether it is personal or professional, shows you have a teachable and humble spirit.

I recently came across this observation about humility and teachability from one of my favorite pundits, James Thurber. It pretty well encapsulates my thoughts: "No one has all the answers, and [James] Thurber posits that pretending otherwise will get you into trouble. He

---

[22] Scott Frost

encourages all generations to remember that curiosity is a sign of respect, and indicates a willingness to learn, and grow, from the presence of outside perspectives."[23]

Finally, these words from the great Green Bay Packers quarterback, Aaron Rogers, exemplify the spirit of these two qualities. "I was in a room for 3 years with a better player than me for the first time in my career and I got to see what greatness looked like up close," Rodgers said. "I got to see the difference between his game and my game — and how I needed to improve. I got to see a leadership style and take some things from it. I was fortunate to play behind Brett [Favre] for three years. I learned a lot of incredible lessons."

Lesson: *"I never lose. I either win or learn."*[24]

Discerning and Insightful

Discernment is a necessary tool for effective leadership, like a hammer is to a carpenter. Briefly, discernment is the ability to look into the fog, or the future, and find a way through. It enables leaders to read people

---

23 https://www.inspiringquotes.com
24 Nelson Mandela

and situations clearly, to forecast probability and act in everyone's best interests.

When the stakes are high, every business or organization wants to follow the person with the track record of being correct in critical moments. It is the soldier who feels uncomfortable advancing to reconnoiter a safe route for the platoon. It is a personnel director who has an uncomfortable feeling about an applicant so they run deeper background checks. It is the CEO who can see through the backslappers and sycophants to select an honest and capable candidate. Discernment addresses uncertainty and finds safety.

Remember the story of Solomon's legendary wisdom when two mothers both claimed the same baby? In a moment of great insight he ordered the baby cut in half so both women would have something to hold. Immediately the real mother abrogated her rights to the child.

Leaders must routinely make hard decisions and a discerning spirit might be the difference between good or great outcomes. As Jesus said, "Look, I am sending you out as sheep among wolves. So be as shrewd as snakes and harmless as doves."[25] That is easier said than done.

---

[25] Matthew 10:6. New Living Translation.

How does one develop discernment? That depends on how much one values truth. I believe discernment is partially intuition, partially information and partially experience, topped off with a large portion of desire to be led by truth. A commitment to being informed allows us to be insightful and embrace our values when it matters most. Prepare yourself enough to trust yourself when it really counts.

Children are not born with discernment and it rarely evidences itself until they have made a few mistakes - and lived to tell about it. Teenagers are notorious for testing boundaries and getting burned, only to try the same thing again. For new young drivers speeding is a real turn-on… until the ticket must be paid. And saddest of all, multitudes of adults driven by emotions or feelings, not discernment and insight, choose the way of short-term enjoyment over long-term life investment. "If the government will pay me not to work, why should I get a job?"

I have taken time to understand the many nuances of discernment and the following is from my first book, *Praying When Prayer Doesn't Work.* "Note that the words concern and discern have a common suffix. When concerned, we worry about challenges, circumstances, cravings, or callings that might disrupt our peace and therefore the order in our souls. The remedy for concern is discernment, the ability to disconnect the links between the realities and the perceptions that concern us."[26]

Mark Twain colorfully describes how that process of finding truth works: "Drag your thoughts away from your troubles ... by the ears, by the heels or any other way you can imagine it." [27]

The battles that help us defeat uncertainty are never easy, but once won, our direction is plainly established. Discernment and insight are invaluable tools for leaders as they clear the way through the dark forest of uncertainty. One can be used as a machete and the other as a lantern. Trying to lead without discernment and insight only takes you in circles when your goal is getting out.

> **Lesson:** *"We delight in the beauty of the butterfly, but rarely admit the changes it has gone through to achieve that beauty."*[28]

---

[26] Praying When Prayer Doesn't Work. Jack Corbin Getz. iUniverse Press. 2010. Page 63
[27] Ibid Page 242
[28] Mary Angelou

Why Leadership Skills Are Important?

- Staying positive.
- High productivity.
- Good communication skills.
- Motivation.
- Open mind.
- Empathy.
- Humility.
- Understanding.

www.visualposting.com

Chapter Four

BUILDING A LEADERSHIP LEGACY

LEADERSHIP SHOULD NOT be undertaken on a whim just because it looks like a good gig. It is often highly rewarding but to enjoy those rewards, it may also demand more than expected. Certainly there are those naturals who understand the cost and prepare themselves by obtaining the necessities to lead through sacrifice, education and good experience.

Few leaders inherit their positions but instead work their way into situations enabling them to demonstrate their skills and aptitude for advancement. Good leaders start out with a desire or calling to lead and that sense is only enhanced by success.

My watercolor painting skills did not come easily or cheaply, but after I reached a point of competency, my courage and confidence allowed me to both teach others and sell my work. My desire to paint was my gift but my determination to improve is why I have succeeded.

While the need for new and capable leadership is present in any undertaking, expediency can quickly compromise best practices and elevate social, cultural or structural quotas like attempting to force square pegs into round holes: "We need more diversity in our leadership portfolio so who can we advance?"

Turning businesses, churches, schools, the military and government into short-term social-engineering experiments is a sure way to court long-term disaster.

Why? Filling quotas short-circuits the process of leadership development in favor of political expediency. Attempting to make everyone happy is not part of successful stewardship. Making a leader to satisfy a quota of a particular constituency or overcoming someone's sense of marginalization may be popular with cultural subsets and may be one way to keep the peace, but it is not always the best way to run a business. At best it is a short-term solution to long-term needs, and it sacrifices tomorrow's best for tranquility today.

Creating a positive leadership legacy ought to matter a great deal to any group, just as it did to Henry VIII in the sixteenth century. Organizations and businesses that focus mostly on social or external pressures for their succession planning may be creating a long, slow, deadly erosion ultimately destroying the great accomplishments of the past.

Organizations of any size ought to focus on subjects such as these to both develop and retain their most valued employees:

- Prioritizing employee development
- Facilitating a sense of purpose
- Caring about employees
- Considering employee opinions
- Focusing on employee strength[29]

A more proactive approach to create a lasting leadership legacy avoids the pressure of expedient quotas and focuses on making leadership available to all, allowing performance to trump all other factors.

---

29 Harvard Business Review, January 21, 2022.

The following from the Harvard Business Review presents five invaluable conversation starters with which employees - both with and without observable leadership aspirations - may be engaged.

1. How would you like to grow within this organization?
2. Do you feel a sense of purpose in your job?
3. What do you need from me to do your best work?
4. What are we currently not doing as a company that you feel we should do?
5. Do you have the opportunity to do what you do best every day?

The Dalai Lama understands the principle of building a lasting legacy and said, "Reason well from the beginning and then there will never be any need to look back with confusion and doubt." Anything less than consistent good personnel practices and thoughtful succession planning systems to identify and coach potential leaders, regardless of their gender or race, is failed leadership.

The foolishness of filling leadership quotas based on anything but one's record, capacity and potential is easily seen in the sport of fishing. Both the law and common sense dictate that we cannot keep every fish that bites on the hook. Some are too small or not good for eating or mounting. If your goal is to eat bass for supper, a catfish will not do. Taking a string of four inch sunfish to a fishing contest weigh-in is foolish at best, and pretending a catfish is a bass, or a minnow is a trophy fish, does not make sense either.

Forty years ago I was under the leadership of a pioneering single woman leader. Some thought she gained her position only because she was a woman. In truth, she turned out to be a competent leader. At first she was an oddity because of her gender. Her rigid style alienated as many as not, but with time she adapted to her role and her experience and ability to produce under pressure validated her leadership. Today those who worked with her would say she is an heroic figure, breaking the organization's glass ceiling, making women's leadership assignments routine, not unique.

It is the responsibility of current leaders to prepare future leaders. Creating an atmosphere where capacity and performance trump every other factor when considering future advancement must prevail. In the process of mentoring, training and tutoring those who demonstrate both the ability to learn and lead, one's race, gender, physical condition or age ought not limit inclusion. Conversely, to ensure long-range credibility, no one should be advanced based solely on any of those factors. A level playing field is all anyone expects, or deserves.

> *Lesson*: *"Ability is nothing without opportunity."* [30]

---

[30] Napoleon Bonaparte.

Chapter Five

MOTIVATIONS

SOME BELIEVE THEY ought to pursue leadership. Others believe they need to. And still others sense leadership is pursuing them. It has always been a bit of a mystery why people want to lead, especially in difficult times, but as I said in the Introduction and Forward, I think that regardless of the compensation, leadership in any age, including today, is like taking a Sunday stroll in a mine field.

So what motivates people to desire leadership? What is so attractive about it? Don't some say the costs are greater than the rewards, and potential hazards not worth the risks?

I recently heard a big-city mayor honestly answer the question of why he ran for office saying "This is where the power is." He understood that only with power could he hope to address the complex problems that existed in his city. Like many public servants, the desire to lead is more about the ability to direct change than financial perks. For example, by design the President of the United States makes $400,000 a year, a paltry sum for the work expected. For many, leadership is a means to an end, not an end in itself.

I am sure some claim a need (demand-side motivation), because they want to help, to serve, to fix, or create necessary change. That is all well and good, but beneath even the most altruistic motives is a reward (supply-side motivation). Like the mayor who coveted power, many like the perks that accompany leadership, especially in big business. I am not suggesting that everyone who wants to lead for this reason is selfish or mercenary but I believe whatever is second on the motivation list to self-interest is not very close. An honest, soul searching appraisal of motives to lead may conclude that "What's in it for me?" usually outweighs "How can I help?"

I can imagine some of my service-directed friends jumping up in protest to this odd perception, but when I speak of *Compensation* I include a Pandora's box of valid reasons people are motivated by both obvious and less obvious supply side perks. Money, nice cars, authority or status are not always considered self-interest compensation. Remember, looking out for oneself is not always a negative but is often necessary.

To be fair, when leadership's hard realities and responsibilities are encountered, those gaudy benefits may quickly lose some of their appeal. Today's economy has created demand-side paradise for employees. Even hourly wage earners can demand non-monetary compensation such as stay-at-home work, child care assistance, flex schedules and reduced work weeks. Compensation is not just how much money you make but how much your work environment contributes to your joy and wellbeing.

Jeff Abbott, CEO of Ivanti, the company behind a survey relating to employee's changing employment aspirations, reveals some startling trends. "In the latest revealing survey of 4,510 office workers from several countries, seven in 10 respondents indicated that they'd pass up a promotion in favor of the opportunity to work from anywhere, any time. That's an eye-popping number, and one that leaders would be wise to pay attention to."(Connect to the full article link in footnote below.)[31]

---

[31] inc.com Marcelo Schwantes. 70 Percent of Employees Are Saying 'No, Thanks' to a Promotion. Here's What They Want Instead

The late coach John Madden, American football icon, said at his Hall of Fame induction ceremony that he was enabled by others to "play" his whole life, so everything he did was fun. At age 70 he admitted "I never worked a day in my life!" suggesting that his great success and fame were the byproducts of doing what he loved.

Our eldest daughter Jodie is an underpaid public school speech therapist who could use - and deserves - fifty percent more money. But the sad realities of public school compensation do not stop her from cherishing her interactions with her "little people" who think she is nothing short of an angel. She loves telling us stories about how her kids make her happy and, we add, how much good she does for them.

While money is critical for everyone, developing a sense of self-worth and living a peaceful, happy, well-ordered life are of even greater value. It is probably true that money does not buy happiness, but when Clarence the angel said, "No, we don't use money in Heaven", George Bailey responded, "Oh yeah, that's right. I keep forgetting. Comes in pretty handy down here, bub!"[32]

---

[32] It's A Wonderful Life. Liberty Films . 1947

Ideally, everyone should work inside the happy bubble of sufficient money and realized values. Feeling the good balance of these two dynamics is possibly the ultimate compensation. Some can serve a lifetime doing hands-on productivity with no desire to get higher up the pyramid because all they desire is being provided.

Contented workers balance their need for money with an ability to use their best talents/training in a productive setting. If you live to work you may get more cash, position or perks, but you may also be less content than if you work to live. Someone wisely said, I've learned that making a living is not the same thing as making a life. Today in the realities of the employee-driven market, workers are allowed to pursue lifestyle issues, balancing work and home more than ever before.

Those who work to live, can pursue their hobbies, travel, participate in groups and find strength in their faith-communities, all things that money can not buy. Considering such freedoms and residuals ought to be part of any vocation. There is more to success than money.

Compensation - External Motivations

I once had an affable boss who welcomed me to a leadership position saying there were at least three good things about being a leader: "You will always have a parking spot. You will always have a reserved seat and they never begin a meeting until you are there!" Looking back, I can happily say he was right about all three of these practical positional perks.

We all know that in any endeavor there are highly motivated individuals willing to do anything required to raise their forms of compensation, and this is certainly understandable. In fact, it is often commendable if they do not sell their souls to do it. Even the humble monk may aspire to leadership in his monastery after hearing the leaders' mattresses are more comfortable than his. Remember, compensation can be anything that is an external motivator to improve your position.

A 2004 study by researcher Ted Kolditz looked at leadership motivations in military students. In it Kolditz asks, "Can it be simply about perks, power, position or purpose? One of the most telling questions you can ask someone in any kind of leadership role is what motivates them to be a better leader. Some will say it's to enhance their personal effectiveness, or that leading is an expected part of their professional development."[33]

---

33 Hbr.org Harvard Business Review Tom Kolditz July 22, 2014. Why You Lead Determines How Well You Lead

Certainly the external compensation of cash-related benefits are forms of motivation. More is expected of those who determine the bottom line or the stock value, so more is received. I have no doubt that people are highly motivated by the amount of their paycheck every other week. Not many care much about the size of their Christmas ham, but everyone cares about their income.

It might be too obvious to say that the law of supply and demand works quite well in the for-profit world. In fact, since leadership is needed in every organization, the same rules apply to operations like cartels, organized crime, and both rogue and well-established governments. When demand is high, supply pays very well.

So the first motivation for seeking leadership is *External Compensation*. It is a good thing to seek higher responsibility with its accompanying accountability and stress, as long as the pay reflects the personal cost to be there.

Calling - Internal Motivation

In addition to external motivations, there is a large world of internal motivations that in many cases supersedes money. Those who work for non-profit organizations, churches and even the military do not become social workers, teachers, pastors, corporals or counselors if they plan to get rich. They work for something more important, their values.

Winston Churchill had no need of more money, a better mattress or a finer vehicle. He was clearly an exceptional man created for his unique opportunity. His noble upbringing, his unparalleled grasp of British history, his notable record of civil service, including his position as the once failed head of the admiralty, and his legendary stubbornness made him a square peg for a square hole.

Again, Tom Kolditz reveals the essence of Churchill and others motivated by an internal calling to lead. "Others may say that they lead because of a sense of leader identity, purpose, or personal obligation to serve their organization and the people with whom they work. Many will proffer a mix of internal, motivations (like pay or career progression) and more intrinsic, internal rationales (like the obligation to serve)."[34]

Motivated leaders believe they have the right stuff to make a difference, even to the point of claiming a specific and mystical calling to a cause. They have the

---

34 Ibid

conviction that they ought to lead and can lead as well or better than others they work for - or with.

From Mother Teresa to Bill Gates, every leader is partially motivated by something internal. Remember, compensation and motivation are not always tangible. Someone wisely observed that the most important things in life are not things.[35]

A *calling* to lead may or may not be spiritual or mystical in nature. In fact, many times, calling is little more than a thoughtful *response* to a need, enabled by the wedding of competence and ongoing commitment.

Conscription - Circumstantial Motivation

There is a third motivational category which may be considered involuntary and external in nature. Perhaps the best example of this is seen in the world of sports. Most college teams select team captains annually. Coaches encourage this because it identifies natural leaders and makes communication between the staff and the team both efficient and credible.

The voting process is not an election *per se* because players do not conduct traditional campaigns for votes. Instead they are selected by teammates because they

---

35 Anthony J. D'Angelo. www.Brainyquote.com

exhibit desired leadership qualities. In other words, some leaders earn the honor of being elected because they perform consistently and exhibit the team values in routine and exceptional settings. The team is saying they want these peers to represent and empower them to keep everyone moving in the right direction.

Another apt illustration of being chosen to lead by circumstances is that which takes place in war. It does not take long for captains to identify naturally talented sergeants, and for sergeants to identify leaders among those trained to follow them. Good leaders were all at some point good followers. In war, gaining a place of leadership is not anyone's primary goal. Peak performance, survival and victory are.

Some individuals, who in the routine performance of their duties, see a leadership gap, and like air finds a vacuum, they fill it. This phenomenon begs the question "Are leaders born or developed?" Coach Vince Lombardi, never one to mince words, says quite clearly, "Leaders are made, they are not born. They are made by hard effort, which is the price which all of us must pay to achieve any goal that is worthwhile."[36]

---

36 BrainyQuote.com

I agree with the coach but suggest some people are born with a temperament or personality conducive to leadership. I believe effective leading is similar to effective teaching. Not everyone who stands in front of a group and speaks is a good teacher. It takes more than information transfer to transfer information. Sometimes it takes performance and an iron will to communicate at any cost.

My father was a grade school drop out in the tough days of the Great Depression. At a very young age, he was the eldest son in a mostly fatherless family, and was expected to be the man of the house and by hook or by crook forage food for the family of eight. Despite that rough start he used his natural leadership abilities among his friends, and as an adult received the highest civilian award the Boy Scouts of America can bestow, the Silver Beaver, presented by no less than the governor of Illinois. As Booker T. Washington learned in his life, "Success is to be measured not so much by the position that one has reached in life as by the obstacles which he has overcome."

His role as leader and teacher did not come in the traditional way but was literally foisted upon him by cruel circumstances. General Electric's CEO Jack Welch did not know my father but his words make me wonder if he did: "Before you are a leader, success is all about growing yourself. When you become a leader, success is all about growing others."

At our father's funeral both my brother and I incredibly used the same quote to describe his life. "Success is not how far you go, but how far you go from where you started."

That mysterious "it" that some possess is sometimes seen in individuals with unusual personalities, charisma, positive energy and the innate capacity to lead parades, unlike those who find a parade and jump to the front of it.

The "need to lead syndrome" reminds me of a man who was once my immediate supervisor. For some reason my wife asked him about gaining his position, and instead of drenching us in pious faux humility, he honestly answered, "If it comes down to me or someone else, I choose me." How refreshing and how revealing his words were! His response was pragmatic - and honest - two rare commodities absent in far too many ineffective leaders.

Having touched on the three primary motivations to lead, it is now time to present my visual aid about WHY people want to become leaders. To this point we have examined examples of people who chose to lead, what motivates people to pursue leadership and what it takes to mount the leadership platform in the 21st century. This pyramid graph is almost completely about *perception* versus *reality*, and hopefully to feel the heartbeat of this book through it.

The Pyramid Chart

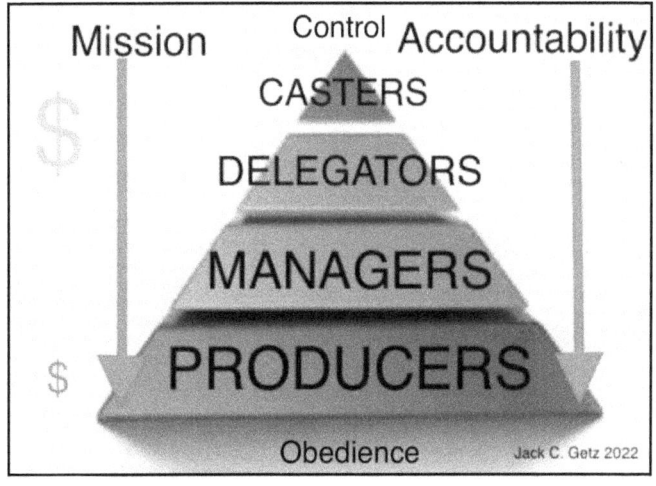

Chapter Six

THE PYRAMID: WHY ORGANIZATIONS ATTRACT LEADERS PYRAMID - PART ONE

THE PYRAMID CHART on the previous page is a visual aid to illustrate my text. The diagram deals with both the *perception* and the *reality* of WHY people want to lead. Although not complicated, it takes a minute to see what it illustrates.

In short, it is a visual explanation of WHY people tend to believe it is better to be a leader than a follower. All of the alluring images of leadership appear at the top of this pyramid. Compensation is greater, control originates there and mission trickles down from above. Conversely, the bottom of the pyramid is occupied by those who take orders, give service and receive less tangible compensation. Interestingly, only this week, I came across Leo Tolstoy's ideas of his four perceived levels of leadership: 'Some men write the laws [Casters], others apply them [Delegators]; a third set drill men and habituate them to discipline [Managers]...a fourth set - the people who are disciplined commit all kinds of deeds [Producers]..." (My categories bracketed)[37]

To begin, take note of the downward vertical arrows. It is important to notice that they point one way (downward), not two ways, indicating a gravitational pressure from the top down. That is perhaps a simplified - possibly cynical - view of how organizational leadership works. Perhaps now is a good time to explain these pyramid symbols further.

Mission

Mission speaks to the heart of any organization, business, charity, military unit or government. The mission statement is a succinct, memorable, sometimes catchy statement regarding the purpose for which something exists. It is not a goal or an objective, but a banner under which the army marches, the business operates or the charity thrives.

---

37 Include Me Out! Colin Morris. Abingdon Press. Page 93.

One memorable example of a mission statement I recall was presented by President John F. Kennedy on May 25, 1961. That day he told Congress "…this nation should commit itself to achieving the goal, before the decade is out, of landing a man on the Moon and returning him safely to the earth."

His mission statement was simple, time sensitive and measurable. Anyone in the space business knew what to do, when to do it and how to know when it was complete. The details of how to achieve a group's mission are secondary issues. Operational outcomes are detailed in goals and objectives, and if someone ever wonders if an action or direction is necessary, they may simply view it through the lens of the mission statement.

Elon Musk kept Tesla's mission statement simple but still poignant saying they exist "To accelerate the world's transition to sustainable energy". And retail giant Walmart chose the simplest words imaginable to convey their purpose to be in business: "To save people money so they can live better."

A clear mission statement engrained in a group's psyche gives the reason to exist. Mission accomplishment is the number one priority of every organization. End of story.

The downward direction of the mission arrow simply implies that the responsibility for mission clarity comes from the top of the organization. The responsibility for mission accomplishment is the primary purpose of those down the chain of command. The hands-on part of mission delivery is achieved by those closer to the bottom of the pyramid. They get to make the widgets, sell the product, cook the meals, run the store and render the service.

Accountability

On the other side of the pyramid to *Mission* is the equally important arrow of *Accountability*. When anyone lacks accountability, it is almost certain they will eventually experience difficulties. Many mighty leaders have fallen from a lack of accountability because it is extremely difficult to confront or question one's leaders. Since self-correcting is unreliable, good leaders are wise to balance themselves by opening communication paths to themselves.

We start learning about accountability as toddlers in the safety of our home. "Momma said no!" are powerful words to a child, especially if momma consistently and gently enforces the rules and rewards for behavior.

There is a concise definition of accountability found in The Merriam Webster Dictionary that sheds valuable light on the issue. It says accountability is "an <u>obligation</u> or <u>willingness</u> to accept responsibility or to account for one's actions." I underlined two important words that are the springboard for much deeper consideration: "obligation" and "willingness".

Both are positive qualities in the work force, but I see them as opposite poles on the continuum of accountability. Obligation and duty anchor one end of the line with willingness and joy the other. Certainly the primary concern of any undertaking is that the job gets done. But if given the choice, I hope that willingness and joy will trump obligation and duty in the workplace.

One of my long held beliefs suggests that choice is what differentiates joy and drudgery. When mission is accomplished by people with choices, not simply duty (or worse, fear) the light of productivity glows brighter.

When any organization appears to be failing in their mission delivery, the natural instinct of top leadership assumes that someone below is the cause. Maybe the widgets are being made incorrectly or painted the wrong color resulting in falling company sales.

But if the flaw exists at the top, there is seemingly less accountability and more grace spread around the office. Those higher on the pyramid have more ability to cover their own deficiency and determine their own fate. But truthfully, they are more accountable for the ship's success, although it does not always seem that way to those down in the engine room. Leadership guru Stephen Covey easily coined this truth saying, "Accountability breeds response-ability."[38]

One good measure of how corporate accountability works is illustrated by a question an executive coach friend uses with his clients: "Ask yourself to calculate the relative costs to the business when you make a mistake, then compare that to the cost incurred when the boss makes a mistake." Little more needs to be said about how accountability really works, but as long as the perception exists that it is better up there than down here, the arrow points down. Remember, the point of this chart is to demonstrate WHY people *think* it is better to be the captain and not a deck hand.

Control and Obedience

The words *Control* and *Obedience* on the upper and lower edges of the pyramid chart are relative terms. The pyramid *implies* the presence of control and obedience changes with one's position on the chart. Often it *appears* there is only one place where obedience is a choice, and that is at the top, and one place where obedience is routinely required, and that is at the bottom.

---

[38] Seven Habits of Highly Effective People. https://www.brainyquote.com/quotes/stephen_covey_636497

For example, the IBM Code of Conduct is an integral part of working there. Note their remarkable level of control over not only their employees but also their vendors: "This Code of Conduct defines the minimum standards of business conduct and business practices with which IBM expects you to comply in regards to your business relationship with International Business Machines Corporation (or one or more of its subsidiaries) …If applicable laws and regulations are more permissive than this Code of Conduct, you are expected to comply with this Code of Conduct. If applicable laws and regulations are more restrictive, you must always comply with those legal requirements."[39]

At one time their strictly enforced dress code set the standard for all business attire. It was called the IBM look. But later dot com companies thumbed their noses at Big Blue's symbols of control and acceptable attire by virtually tearing the dress code page from their employee manual. Their reasoning was that comfortable clothes allowed for a relaxed and creative workplace.

Along with the vanishing employee-driven dress codes went other practices. Soon even conservative organizations started loosening control over some normally protected personnel areas. For example, the dress code for

---

39 https://www.ibm.com/partnerworld/program/code-of-conduct

most organizations has morphed from highly regulated semi-uniform attire to more casual garb. "Casual Fridays" attempt to show the workforce that management was in tune with their needs, while still controlling the rest of the week. Traditional Victorian standards said "Clothes makes the man". But like most things Victorian, they have morphed into today's relaxed standard: "Whatever, man!"

Regarding the pyramid, I theorize that higher downward directed control is essential because that's how mission is achieved: everyone rowing together. The leaders believe that rules are important, policies matter, upward reporting is expected and accountability is king. Yet in companies where high creativity is valued, there are often fewer policies about clothes, office hours or sick days, yielding to the bottom line need to produce the perfect widget or deliver the best service through employees empowered with more choice than in traditional settings.

The control atmosphere is thinner at the top, another reason why many aspire to be there. From the top, strict obedience to rules, policies, standards and daily expectations is seemingly exchanged for more freedom, fewer peers, autonomy and greater decision making ability.

This perception may exist because the view decreases with each step down the pyramid. Big picture issues coming from on high do not concern *Producers* as much as their immediate needs for adequate compensation, safety, opportunity and consistently applied policies.

Compensation

Two notable features of the pyramid chart are the two dollar signs. Their relative size represents the difference between the *observable compensation* for those at the extreme ends of the scale. Whatever the reality, they suggest those at the top drive paid-off Teslas while those at the bottom drive 60 month same-as-cash Fords.

The subject of *Compensation* has already been addressed so all we need say here is that the relative size of the two dollar signs tells the story. The perception of greater rewards accrued at the top is accurate. But the perception that by reaching the top all will be green is not quite true. Debt increases along with income for many because the opportunity to buy bigger and better is always tempting.

Conversely, not everyone at the bottom is debt strapped, but given the fact that the average credit debt in America is always increasing implies that debt is a serious factor in the lives of most workers. Perhaps the power of consumerism and the delights of leisure pursuits have more allure than they ought, but finding personal happiness - at the price of accruing personal debt - suggests there are more important values at play in the workplace than money.

What people **THINK** leadership is:

- Telling people what to do

THE HABIT
STRATEGIST

What **LEADERSHIP** really is:

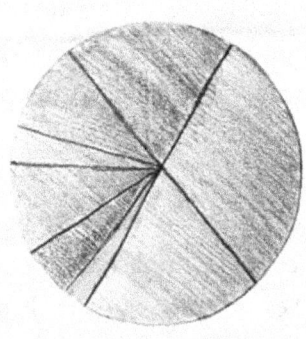

- Integrity
- Cast a vision
- Use of influence
- Use of power
- Praise your team
- Self-awareness
- Listen first and speak last
- Empathy

Chapter Seven

LEADERSHIP PERCEPTIONS AND REALITIES: WHY ORGANIZATIONS ATTRACT LEADERS PYRAMID - PART TWO

LOOK AT THE pyramid again and note the four levels labeled *Producers, Managers, Delegators and Casters.* Clearly they are not of equal volume and each strata is in a symbiotic relationship to those it touches. That means the bottom level has the broadest line of interaction with the next higher section, and *Managers* and *Delegators* have two interface relationships, illustrating their middle management status.

Simply put, the pyramid serves two functions. First, it suggests a functional hierarchy. There are bosses and laborers with differing functions. Second, it clearly illustrates the *perception* that being at the top is more desirable than being at the bottom. It is a visual representation that answers the recurring question of this book, WHY do people want to be leaders?

We all know leaders representing big and small businesses, politics, schools, churches, non-profits, philanthropy, and community organizations. Some are flag wavers who motivate through enthusiasm, others are quiet, cerebral and efficient. Unfortunately others lead through intimidation or unreasonable daily accountability. I had one boss who called all his department heads every night after 9:00 pm to quiz them about the day's production. Then each morning a newly typed to-do list was on their desk awaiting their attention. I also had a boss who told me if I did not hear from him to just keep doing what I was doing. Then one day he fired me because I was not doing what he wanted me to.

Fortunately, the majority of my leaders, and those I knew, were reasonable people who pragmatically undertook their roles with humility and paid the price required of them to lead. Obviously, not everyone leads the same way, so it is impossible to select one person like a Churchill, a Napoleon, a Nick Saban, a Mao

Zedong or even a Mother Teresa as the prototype. All served their purposes effectively and none would have been nearly as notable in a different field. Imagine Napoleon trying to serve the poverty stricken outcasts in Calcutta/Kolkata or Mother Teresa leading an army into war.

All organizations are comprised of people with different skill sets and leadership capacities. It has to be that way or nothing would get done. *Producers*, *Managers*, *Delegators* and *Casters* all address their roles as part of the whole. In math class we learned that the whole is the sum of its parts, so the better a leader increases the buy-in from the parts, the more successful the enterprise. A great organization is not great only because it has a highly credentialed leadership team, but because everyone feels like a stakeholder in the work.

It is important to note that everyone on the pyramid, regardless of their level, has routine leadership opportunities and responsibilities. So a good child care worker is acting in all four levels in their center every day. And both the sailor and the admiral exhibit all the leadership levels on the pyramid within their sphere of influence. The entrepreneurs who feel more effective and motivated outside the structure of a larger enterprise must be all things on the pyramid or their ventures will quickly fail.

I suggest that most people have aspirations to grow in both capacity and compensation. So those who have a desire to improve must choose one of two paths. One is to aspire to be elevated up the pyramid and the other is to become better at what they do where they are, without regard for upward mobility. Unfortunately for them, some never realize their dreams, or fail if they do, and the Peter Principle kicks in, "…they rise to a level of respective incompetence."

NOTE: I urge you to read the "children's" book *Hope for the Flowers* by Trina Paulus to further understand the timeless truths behind the nature of the desire to climb to the "top". [40]

Producers

When I speak of *Producers*, I refer to those individuals who touch the mission daily. One easy way to visualize this group is through the franchise structure of a business. The home office supervises the manager, who may be the local owner, who supervises the producers who deliver the mission to the customers. This franchise concept is seen regularly in places like restaurants, the post office, national charities, churches, grocery stores, schools and manufacturing operations.

---

40 Hope For The Flowers. Trina Paulus. Paulist Press. 1972.

I found a good working definition of the role of *Producers* in the book *Hope For the Flowers:* "Tell me, sir, what is a butterfly?" "It's what you are meant to become. It flies with beautiful wings and joins the earth to heaven. It drinks only nectar from the flowers and the seeds of love from one flower to another. Without butterflies the world would soon have few flowers." [41]

I suggest that *Producers* are the caterpillars who become butterflies. They pollinate the world with the organization's mission to produce the flowers. *Producers* are by necessity the street level ambassadors/achievers supported by the others in the organizational hierarchy above. They make up the group who produce or sell the product/service to the consumer/client/customer. They render hands-on service and model the group's brand to the public.

Producers routinely carry the water for the organization and yet they are the most supervised, audited and regulated individuals in the structure. They may be clock punchers who feed the hungry, build the widget, flip the burgers, and turn the lights off at night, but not always.

Producers are not simply low level organizational lackeys. They can be well-paid professionals who raise or

---

41   Ibid

manage money, sell the product, teach mathematics, perform surgery or supervise a large department, but all mission level hands-on workers are members of the *Producer* class on the pyramid.

A successful *Producer* is content, not driven to prove anything to others, often revered and respected more than their leaders. The life long *Producer* may have eschewed the opportunity to ascend the *Pyramid* but despite that, they find contentment and satisfying compensation in playing their role faithfully.

Producers are the foundation of the organization that determines its longevity and success. Jesus, a classic producer, taught about the critical nature of foundations. "Anyone who listens to my teaching and follows it is wise, like a person who builds a house on solid rock. Though the rain comes in torrents and the floodwaters rise and the winds beat against that house, it won't collapse because it is built on bedrock. But anyone who hears my teaching and doesn't obey it is foolish, like a person who builds a house on sand. When the rains and floods come and the winds beat against that house, it will collapse with a mighty crash."[42] I believe it is fair to suggests the same fate awaits any organization that neglects or marginalizes its *Producer* base.

---

42 Matthew 7:24-29 New Living Translation. Tyndale Publishing

Managers

Immediately above the *Producers* are *Managers* who routinely interface with *Producers*, and report information to *Delegators*. *Managers* provide *Producers* with direct business services, both in professional level support and remedial management oversight. They are one level removed from direct mission implementation. *Managers* are often former *Producers* who chose, or were chosen, to occupy a place of lower middle management, often to pursue a specific specialty or interest.

Managers have some oversight and supervisory authority. But more often they supplement or resource, hoping to offset unnecessary distractions or organizational encumbrances for *Producers*. They may be bookkeepers, auditors, program specialists, foremen, group leaders, statisticians, reviewers, or grant writers. *Managers* are often leaders-in-training, called upon to do the bidding of those above. Because of their unique place on the pyramid, some choose to make the best of it where they are, others long for the action below at the *Producer* level, and a few aspire to move up to the next level, *Delegators*.

Delegators

Approaching the upper levels of the *Pyramid* are those placed between top leadership *Casters* and lower level *Managers;* they are called *Delegators*. They have one report up and two oversights down.

They are regional representatives who possess increased authority, greater responsibility and therefore higher compensation. As they ascend, they also separate from hands-on *Mission*. They probably once excelled at the lower levels, and believe their role is to model, encourage, resource, interpret, discipline and sometimes strut a bit.

Suppose the chief *Delegator* at the Acme Chicken Plucking Company feels it is important to send a message to her staff that she is mission sensitive. To deliver her message, she believes she should personally take a turn at plucking chickens. The experience is anything but rewarding but she hopes her presence will signal that she is mission sensitive, in sync with the workers, and practically involved in mission despite her envied position. Certainly, her gesture is noted and possibly appreciated, but while her limited foray into production has benefit, it does not give her credibility as a chicken plucker. I wonder if she understood Peter Drucker's adage, "Management is doing things right; leadership is doing the right things."

Certainly there is no shame in moving upward. The work at the top is critical, but for our purposes, the possibility of upward mobility is one of the major reasons why many *Producers* and *Managers* want to become *Delegators*. While most do not have the capacity to move to the top, many have a "calling" to see what's up there.

I once had a *Delegator* boss who proudly said he managed to clear his desk of the day's work by afternoon coffee break. What he did not say was he simply delegated his work to others, mostly me, by 3:00 PM. That way he could get a early start to beat the Chicago rush hour traffic. I soon wanted to become a *Delegator*.

Understanding something of the role of *Delegators* in the leadership structure, this is a good time to open the gilded door leading to the realm where maximum power, compensation and privilege reside.

Casters

This section has the key to the executive suites, a place where very few have the opportunity to enter, but those who do soon experience the weight and the glory of ultimate responsibility, authority and compensation. Part of the allure of the upper level of the pyramid relates to the diminishing number of individuals who work there. With the narrowing of space moving upward there is a corresponding reduction of workers, resulting in an increased compensation package. Because the *Caster* stands alone at the top, they enjoy the benefits of leadership they receive.

Casters were at some point productive *Delegators, Managers and Producers*. They are highly mission minded, accountable for the bottom line and motivated to increase the capacity and productivity of the organization. They speak clearly and easily about the nature of the group's work and usually model the organization's highest values. They are industrious and endowed with most, if not all, of the *Leadership Minimums* outlined in Chapter Three.

Casters understand the differences between a simple vision and mission accomplishment. They see things that others do not and manage pragmatically to get the job done. Ideally, they know how to communicate well with all stakeholders and are comfortable with and around power. They score when others fumble and they insure the deal is closed. In short, a *Caster's* hands-on involvement in mission may be evident only in their words and decisions, but not in their routine, yet they are ultimately responsible for it.

The *Caster's* purpose is to cast the vision, issue directives, set the pace, represent the organization, develop strategic plans, directly oversee, discipline and motivate *Delegators*, enact policy, and efficiently steer the ship to port. *Casters* do not work in the galley, arrange the deck chairs or play shuffleboard with the passengers.

They are charged to miss the icebergs, and arrive in port safely and on time.

In today's challenging leadership climate, *Casters* are forced into new roles that hardly resemble the old days when edicts were passed down from the top without much argument. As we noted earlier, the employment tables are turned and the top has in essence become the bottom. Now employees often hold the balance of power. So *Casters* must learn to adapt. Much of what they were taught in their traditional MBA training is tempered by the new realities of this period in history. With increasing frequency, the tail is now wagging the dog.

I do not think it is a stretch to suggest that traditional leadership authority is being replaced by compromise, consensus, conscience and coaching. The large bubble of mostly obedient Boomers has passed and now groups like Millennials and others demand answers, reasons and explanations before they will follow. Their calling now, more than ever, is to enable those in their charge while moving the entire organization toward mission accomplishment.

Remember it takes the whole crew for a ship to reach the port. Everyone's role is important, but being the captain is usually thought the best.

SUMMARY AND CONCLUSION

THIS BOOK IS primarily about leadership *Perceptions* and *Realities*. The *Perception* is that being a leader is a great gig. And as we have seen, the compensation for doing it well is both appropriate and appealing. When someone has the authority to distribute the workload, order the troops to charge, delegate responsibility at will, always bat clean up for the "team", and receive the highest compensation, it is hard not to covet their place.

The *Reality* of leadership has been addressed in the preceding pages, so here all I need to do is remind the reader that all that glitters is not gold, especially today. Some have the capacity, the training, the experience and the opportunity to climb to the summit. Because of the value of higher education a good many never need to experience anything below the *Delegator* role. That said, each person in any good organization can find a place where their work and their compensation are a good fit and life can be fulfilling and productive. Such a place is where workers are comfortable with "What they pay for their pay".

Organizations operate as symbiotic organisms. Like a tree, each part - both visible and invisible - is critical to sustaining life and growth. As in nature, no productive part is irreplaceable or redundant, so failure in any of the tree's highly complex system results in its death.

If people in an organization - at any level - fail to do their part for the greater good, they contribute to its withering and possibly its demise. Each person's personal pyramid performance - *Producer* to *Caster* - is critical to success, and coveting a role for any reason other than your capacity to do it better than everyone else, damages mission effectiveness.

Again, Trina Paulus in *Hope for the Flowers* leads us to understand more about the beguiling nature of leadership. She writes a clever fable about two caterpillars, Stripe and Yellow, who one day come to the same conclusion that, "There must be more to life than just eating and getting bigger."

One day they saw a line of caterpillars migrating toward a number of strange pillars. To satisfy their curiosity they joined in and soon learned that no one in line knew any more than they did about the fuss. So they eagerly got in line and headed toward the mysterious pillars.

"Do you know what's happening?" The responses were mostly unhelpful as they blindly migrated. "But what's at the top?" he asked. "No one knows…but it must be awfully good because everybody's rushing there."

After their arduous, long and tiring climb, they eagerly approached the top only to discover the disappointing secret of the pillar: "… [they] heard a tiny whisper from the top: 'There's nothing here at all!' It was answered by another: 'Quiet fool! They'll hear you down the pillar. We're where they want to get. That's what's here!' Stripe felt frozen. To be so high and not high at all! It only looked good from the bottom." [43]

The climb to leadership, to which so many aspire, can be a fickle and disappointing experience. Wherever one works on the pyramid, contentment only comes with mission achievement and ongoing meaningful purpose. *Casters*, *Delegators*, *Managers* and *Producers* each require these things, lest they one day realize too late, like Stripe, "There's nothing here."

---

[43] Hope For The Flowers. Trina Paulas. Paulist Press. New York, New York.1972.

Since so many caterpillars are climbing over each other on those mysterious pillars, it is easy to lose one's purpose and identity and eventually their place. Winston Churchill led his nation to their "finest hour" in the midst of overwhelming odds, yet in the post war election, his party failed to support his bid for re-election and he learned that the descent is much faster than the ascent.

When you are in a business, a government, an army or a non-profit where people feel called to a place at the top, it is natural to look to your self-interests and feel compelled to achieve more. Ideally everyone wants to help attain a desired *Mission*, but sometimes they do not because they have become distracted by where the crowd is going. Losing one's way is called Mission Drift, and as the word drift suggests, it is not lost in a moment, but in a migration.

We learn from experience that finding a place in the world, not on a useless pillar, is a good thing. The dishwasher wants to be a server. The server wants to be a manager, and the manager wants to be an owner. Remember, the destiny of every caterpillar is to become a butterfly, not a leaf-eater forever.

Hopefully, there is always a better deal to be had, a nicer place to work, a bigger responsibility to be claimed and ultimately a more satisfying position to occupy. I would say it is human nature to want to improve, but tragically some forfeit their dreams because of unfortunate barriers to their success.

It is important to note that being on the *Pyramid*, regardless of its size, is a win. Success need not be measured only by one's level on the pyramid. For example, it is more than okay to be a great *Producer*, a competent *Manager,* or a supportive *Delegator*.

I learned long ago from preacher Stewart Briscoe that contentment is living so you do not have to prove anything to anyone. I believe that comparison living is frustrated living. Content individuals understand that success is not always found in moving toward the top, but in doing self-fulfilling work without regard to other's expectations.

As my big business mogul friend Larry says: "People look at me and say they would like what I receive in compensation. They want a title, a nice business card, great trips and an expensive car, but they don't want to pay the price in hours, stress, expectations and accountability that leaders pay every day." Leadership is desirable for many because of the perceived benefits, but truthfully, it is not easy to motivate people to do better, think bigger and contribute only excellence toward mission achievement.

We can learn a great deal about leadership by looking at the bucolic image of shepherds and sheep. First, sheep seem content as long as they are safe and able to eat new grass. Shepherds are most likely content if the sheep are protected and productive. Owners are content when sheep and shepherds continue the cycle of producing desired revenue.

Is it okay to be a sheep? I say yes because their mission is to eat, reproduce, contribute wool and die in old age. How is it being a shepherd? Since sheep can not self-regulate or protect themselves, shepherds are essential. Their life is probably less fulfilling than being a sheep, but it is okay for a while, until something better comes along.

If the shepherd wants to start their own flock things get complicated for the owner. But, like many others, shepherds may fancy a place higher on the *Pyramid* because things look better up there, and chasing wolves or freezing alone on a mountain at night is not everyone's idea of a dream job.

Remember King David in the Bible was relegated to being the family shepherd because he was the youngest son. He was an entry level *Producer* who took every opportunity to learn and develop himself, eventually becoming the nation's heroic *Caster/king*. If shepherd/

Producers plan well, learn the rudiments of the operation, stay diligent and routinely deliver the goods, they ought to learn enough to succeed at higher levels.

I suppose some will read this book and think I am discouraging people from seeking their place near the top. I am pragmatic enough to understand that my words will not dissuade good people from jumping on the leadership ladder, and that's as it should be. My point is not to suggest leadership is unimportant or undesirable, but to emphasize that all that glitters is not gold.

The bottom line is that it takes effective leadership to advance any endeavor. We need good leaders who should reap benefits commensurate with their contributions. And as long as people are motivated and willing to pay the price to lead, there will always be a place for them.

If the boy David wanted to be king before paying the price as a good shepherd, he would have struggled to survive as a king. Leadership exacts a toll, and those who fail to pay it also fail to thrive. Sometimes, like the persistent *Producer* caterpillars, being a bored leaf eater is not bad if it leads to becoming a beautiful butterfly.

THE END

ACKNOWLEDGEMENTS

LARRY ROWLAND'S NAME and his insightful comments about top leadership appear throughout this book. He and I talk on the phone enough that our iron sharpens iron. He was the international *Caster* of a well known financial/reinsurance institution and his stories and insights were invaluable to me, a not for profit *Delegator*. His encouragement to write this book incentivized me to start, and the finished product is largely due to his motivational ways.

Another friend asking not to be named did extensive editing, re-editing, and more editing. Her patience in restarting the process too many times is remarkable, as was her expert editing process.

My wife Barbara is always both my chief cheer leader and my brutal editor. Gracious beyond description, she is the wind beneath my wings now for almost 50 years.

The final product is my responsibility and any errors or inaccuracies are solely my doing, not attributable to any of these three marvelous people.

www.ingramcontent.com/pod-product-compliance
Lightning Source LLC
LaVergne TN
LVHW020448070526
838199LV00063B/4887